FULL CIRCLE

Samantha Sanayhie

BookLeaf Publishing

India | USA | UK

Presentation by *BookLeaf* Publishing

Web: www.bookleafpub.com

E-mail: info@bookleafpub.com

ISBN :9789358361766

First Edition 2021

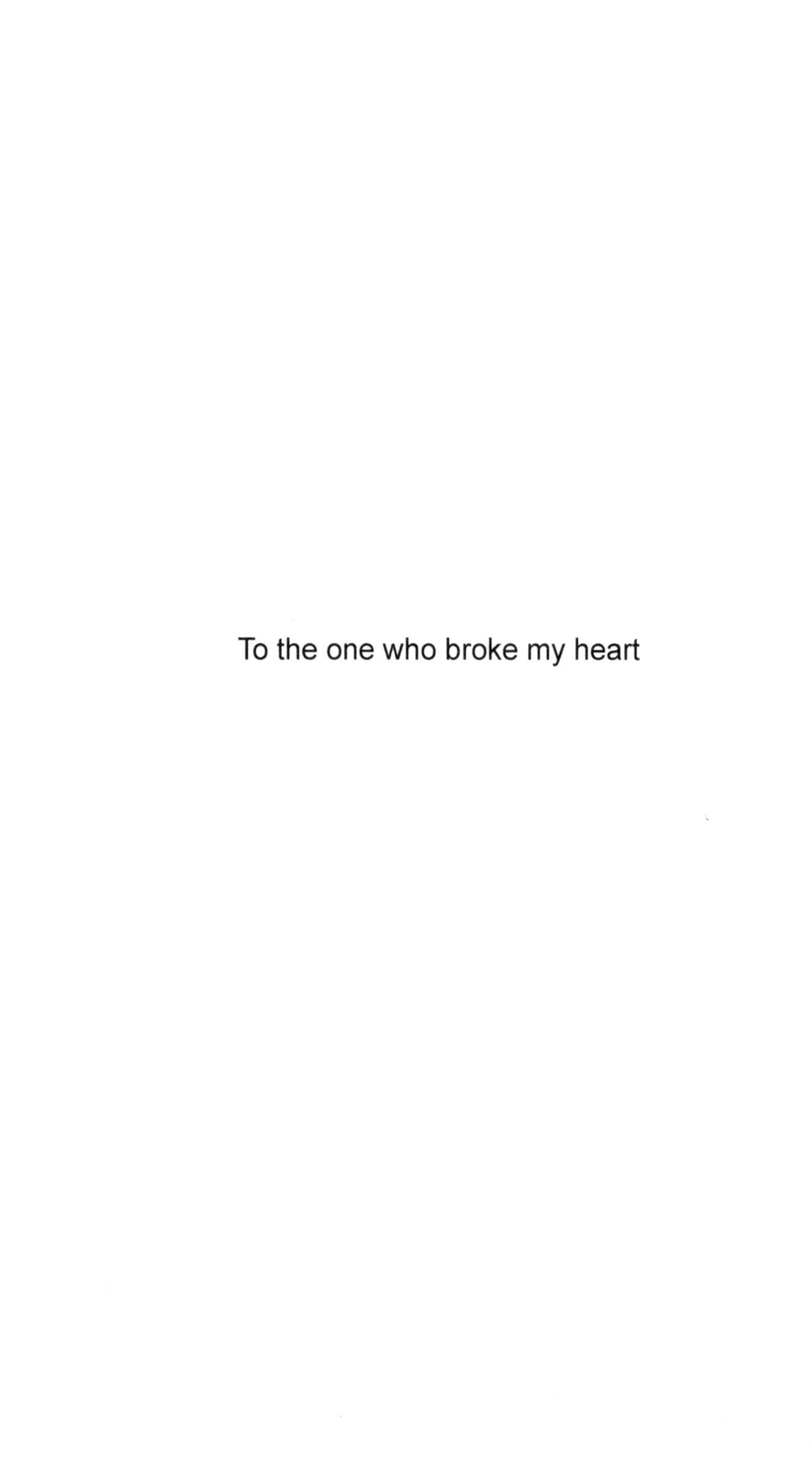

To the one who broke my heart

1.

And there it was.

That laugh.

I love it.

I love that I can make you laugh like that.

And don't even get me started on your smile.

You know,

The one where your eyes crinkle.

God.

It makes me smile just thinking of you,

Smiling down at me,

Laughing with me.

We could be doing anything!

Anything in the world,

And I'd still smile because I'd be with you.

My favourite moments though,

Are when the entire world,

Every detail,

Big and small,

Fades away,

So all that remains is you and I.

You and I,

Against the world.

It's what I love.

2.

Breathtaking.

You take my breath away.

I'm at a loss for words,

Each and every time I see you.

How can someone so good,

So pure,

So breathtaking,

Be with someone like me.

I am oh so lucky,

So happy,

That I am the one,

The one you chose,

Above everyone else.

You came into my life,

like a gust of wind,

And took my breath away.

Breathtaking.

You are breathtaking.

3.

Home isn't a place,

Or a thing,

It's you.

You've become my comfort,

My warmth,

My rock.

You are my home.

If I am ever in need

I know that I can always turn to you.

You keep me anchored and focused,

Something no one before has ever done.

Yet you tickle my curiosity,

Make me want to explore all the doors ahead.

You are my beacon,

That guides me when I am lost.

You are the one that I will always come
back to,

No matter what.

My home is with you,

And I will always know my way home.

4.

Eyes open.

The sun is up.

It's a new day.

A new day with you.

I always want to start my days with you.

Your arm around my waist,

My head against your chest,

Breathing in and out as one.

Not a sound to be heard except the beat
of your heart,

Beneath my ear,

Strong and steady.

These moments right here,

Make all the stress,

The pain,

And the worries worth it,

Because at the end of the day,

When the sun is gone,

Eyes are closed,

I get to be with you.

5.

Love.

A four-letter word.

Short and simple,

Yet the act of love is anything but.

Love.

I love my friends and my family,

But with you it's different.

Love.

I am in love with you.

I'm in love with your smile,

With your hugs,

With your kisses.

I'm in love with your soul,

So young and lively,

Yet quiet and stoic.

Love.

You do crazy things when you're in love.

It's a four-letter word,

Short and simple,

Yet to be in love is anything but.

Love.

I am crazy in love with you.

6.

Is this happiness?

Smiling all day long,

Hand in hand with the one I love.

Is this heaven?

It sure feels like it.

An angel must have heard my prayers
and sent me you.

Or maybe you're an angel in disguise,

Watching over my shoulder,

Offering only love and support.

Is this a dream?

I'd be devastated if it was.

I never want to wake up from you.

I'd stay forever asleep if meant being
with you.

Is this real?

I can touch you,

Hold you,

Feel your warmth,

Your grasp,

Your comforting squeeze,

Silently promising me you'd never leave.

Is this happiness?

Yes.

It most definitely is.

7.

Something is not quite right.

I feel it,

Deep in my bones,

Rattling me.

You're thinking,

Overthinking.

I can tell.

I can read you like a book I've read a million times.

You try to play it off and flip to a new page,

But I know.

You're becoming distant,

Not talking,

Slowly pulling away,

But why?

I don't know.

All I know,

Is that something is not quite right.

8.

What happened?

Did I do this?

Is this my fault?

How can something go from so good to
so bad,

All in one second.

Did I do this?

Is this my fault?

Am I the reason why?

Did I do this!

Did I push you too far?

Did I push you away?

Did I break us?

Did I do this!

Please,

Come back,

I'm sorry.

Did I do this?

Did I destroy everything?

Is this happening because of me?

Is this my fault?

Please!

Just answer me.

Did I do this?

9.

Here I am.

Waiting.

Outside,

In the cold, cold rain.

For you.

For you to come save me,

Save me from drowning,

Drowning in my fear.

Fear of love,

Trust,

And the possibilities.

The possibilities are endless,

Endless ways of hurt,

Of pain,

Pain that turns me numb.

If I love, I feel,

But if I don't feel then I don't get hurt.

Hurt again.

Again you hurt me,

Yet I still trust you,

You,

The one person that I could love forever.

Forever.

I will wait forever,

In the cold, cold rain,

For you.

10.

Do you miss me?

I ask myself that every single day.

Do you miss me?

I know the answer.

You don't.

Why would you?

I hurt you,

But yet I wonder,

Do you miss me?

You hurt me too though,

So much more than I hurt you,

In so many ways

That I lose count.

Do you miss me?

I wonder if I cross your mind,

But why would I?

You've moved on.

Found someone new so fast,

But do I cross your mind?

Do you miss me?

What about when you see me,

Standing there,

Across the room?

Do you think a million things like I do?

Wonder what we'd be doing now if you
didn't walk away,

Wonder if I'm still the same,

Or if I changed,

Do you miss me?

Do you think about everything you told
me?

And how they've all turned into lies.

In a way you deceived me.

I'm so angry,

So hurt,

But still I wonder,

Do you miss me?

Because I miss you.

11.

I'm infected.

Every cell,

And every fiber

That makes up my entire being,

Is infected.

You came,

Entered my life,

And in the blink of an eye,

You left your mark.

It's everywhere,

Even in the tiny little nooks and
crannies.

You took over,

And I didn't see it coming.

But when I realized,

I let you.

I let you invade my life,

My soul,

My heart.

I was sick.

You were my poison,

And yet somehow also my antidote.

You got bored though,

You needed a new host,

To grow,

To expand,

To improve.

So, you left me.

But I am still infected with you.

Your essence is everywhere.

It's toxic,

And no matter what I do to try and rid
you from my being,

You remain.

Yet I don't mind,

I've grown used to it,

This infection.

I find comfort in it,

Even if it is just the ghost of you.

12.

It was just the two of us,

Against the world,

Or so I thought.

Somehow, I ended up all alone.

No more you and I,

No more dynamic duo,

No more perfect pair.

I never saw it coming,

You leaving me on my own,

To carry the weight of the world on my
shoulders.

It all happened so sudden.

One second you were here,

The next you were gone.

I crumbled.

It is me and you and her.

Worlds apart.

I no longer experience those bright,
sunny days,

When we'd get lost in a new adventure.

No.

Now my days are shadowed,

Shadowed with this weight I've
struggled to carry since the day you left.

Now it is you and her,

Somewhere out there,

And now it is just me,

Against all worlds,

All alone,

Hand outstretched,

Waiting,

For it to be you and I once more.

13.

If I disappeared,

Would you even care?

Would you even notice?

Or would it be like a breeze,

Passing by,

Just for a moment?

14.

Tick.

Tock.

What am I doing?

Tick.

Nothing.

Tock.

I am doing absolutely nothing.

I sit here,

Day in,

Day out,

Doing absolutely nothing.

Tick.

Maybe I'm waiting,

But for what?

For you to come back,

To say you made the biggest mistake,

That you miss me, miss us.

Is that what I'm waiting for?

Tock.

But why?

I thought I let it go.

Yet there are still things,

Small things,

That break my heart,

And make me want to go back.

Tick.

You're here.

You still have a hold on me.

I'm haunted by you,

Everything you said,

You did,

Our memories.

Your presence is simply everywhere.

What am I supposed to do?

Tock.

Help.

I'm so lost.

I need you.

NO!

Stop this.

Tick.

I'm in constant turmoil.

Tock.

If I'm over you and don't need you,

Why do I still care,

Still wonder?

Tick,

Tock.

When will this clock stop?

15.

Am I ready?

Ready to move on,

Let go,

Forget about you,

About us,

About all we ever had?

Am I ready?

My friends think I should,

But I don't think I could.

It's true you aren't on my mind all day,

Or every day anymore,

But I still get those glimpses,

That take me back to those moments
we shared.

I could be walking down the street,

Going out to eat,

Or even watching T.V.

And ever so swiftly you're back,

On my mind,

Even if it is only for a moment.

Those glimpses make my heart ache,

But not in the way it did before when I
was painstakingly sad.

I long for us,

Yet I won't reach out to you.

So, am I ready?

My brain tells me I am,

But the way my heart clenches at those
glimpses,

The way I long to be hand in hand,

Making more and more memories,

Tells me I'm not.

Am I ready?

I don't think I am.

16.

Let go.

Be free.

Free from the hurt,

The sadness,

The anger.

Just let it all go.

Now breathe in.

Breathe out.

It's gone.

The weight that was always there,

Resting on your shoulders,

It's gone now.

Again.

Breathe in,

Breathe out.

Look around you,

What do you see?

See the things,

The places,

The people,

That make you happy,

And make you smile,

Despite all that weight.

Focus.

Focus on the light,

Forget the heavy.

Again.

Breathe in,

Breathe out,

Let go.

17.

Strong.

They tell me I'm strong.

Strong because I still faced you every day after.

Strong because I made it.

I made it out of that long,

Dark,

Never-ending tunnel.

Strong.

Some days I don't think I'm strong.

Sure, I don't think of you

Or about us really,

But some days I still wonder about the what ifs.

Maybe that's just curiosity,

But curiosity will always kill the cat.

I know I shouldn't linger

On what could've been,

And focus on what can,

And I am.

Strong.

Maybe I am strong.

I survived.

I survived those tidal waves of pain,

Crashing over and over.

I survived.

Strong.

Maybe I am strong.

I grew,

Grew from our relationship,

From you,

But not just that.

I grew from my mistakes,

Something that you could never do.

Strong.

I am strong.

18.

There you are.

Across the street.

Walking without a care in the world.

There you go,

off somewhere with your friends,

you're gone.

Yet here I am,

All alone,

But that's okay.

I'm okay.

I'm better than okay,

I'm happy.

I see you and nothing.

No pain,

No sadness,

No longing.

I look at you with nothing but content.

Content from our memories,

And the time we had together.

I will always love you,

But I'm ready.

Ready to move forward,

To find myself,

To make myself happy,

Above anyone else.

I'm happy.

This type of happiness is never-ending.

It doesn't come from someone else,

But from within myself.

I can confidently say,

Without an ounce of doubt,

I am happy.

19.

Look up.

There he is.

Look down.

I think he smiled at me.

Nervous.

He makes me nervous,

In all the best ways.

I don't know him,

But I want to.

Look up.

Smile.

Look down.

Did I catch his attention?

I hope so.

I wonder if he notices me the way I
notice him.

Look up.

No! Look down!

He's coming over.

What could he want?

Is my hair okay?

My breath?

Is there something in my teeth?

Do I smell?

Shit! Look up!

Lost.

I am lost in his eyes.

I've never been so close to him.

Every detail,

Big and small,

Has become clear as day.

Beautiful.

He called me beautiful.

Look down.

Smile.

I'm ready.

20.

Life.

It is anything but easy.

Sometimes you get to the high points in
life,

Just to fall back down to the bottom.

But that won't stop you.

It may take weeks,

Months,

Or years,

But you will find you back to the top.

You will ride out those high moments,

For as long as they last,

Remembering the path you took to get
there.

Life.

It's full of highs and lows,

But that's just how it goes.

It's a cycle.

It can be fast,

Or it can be slow,

You can climb,

 Or you can fall.

There's no set time,

Nor direction you may go.

Life.

Before you know it,

You've come full circle.

Whether you find yourself high or low,

Or somewhere in between

That is life.